D0908319

DISCARD

THE REAL
TOM THUMB

by
Helen Reeder Cross

❧❀❧

Illustrations by
Stephen Gammell

FOUR WINDS PRESS ❧ NEW YORK

LIBRARY OF CONGRESS CATALOGING IN PUBLICATION DATA

Cross, Helen Reeder.
  The real Tom Thumb.

  SUMMARY: A biography of the celebrated midget, including his long friendship with P. T. Barnum, his European
travels, and his marriage to tiny Lavinia Warren Bump.

  1. Stratton, Charles Sherwood, 1838–1883—Juvenile literature. 2. Dwarfs—Biography—Juvenile literature. 3. Circus
performers—Biography—Juvenile   literature. [1. Stratton,
Charles Sherwood, 1838–1883. 2. Dwarfs. 3. Circus per-
formers] I. Gammell, Stephen. H. Title.
  GN69.52.S83C76   573'.8 [B]   [92]   80–11447
                    ISBN 0–590–07606–X

❧

PUBLISHED BY FOUR WINDS PRESS

A DIVISION OF SCHOLASTIC MAGAZINES, INC., NEW YORK, N.Y.

TEXT COPYRIGHT © 1980 BY HELEN REEDER CROSS

ILLUSTRATIONS COPYRIGHT © 1980 BY SCHOLASTIC MAGAZINES, INC.

PRINTED IN THE UNITED STATES OF AMERICA

LIBRARY OF CONGRESS CATALOG NUMBER: 80–11447

1 2 3 4 5 84 83 82 81 80

For Amy, Karen, Debbie, and Ned

CHAPTER
1

"I always knew he was smarter than most," his ma would say. Her tiny son was the leading sensation at Barnum's American Museum.

"He's done well for himself—us, too," his pa would add, eyeing the crowds that swarmed past the box office, eager to see Tom Thumb perform.

His parents had named him Charles Sherwood Stratton, after his two grandpas. His father's name was Sherwood, too. Once a military man, he was a carpenter when Charles was born on January 4, 1838.

The Strattons were poor then. They lived in a small cottage on Dutch Lane in Bridgeport, Connecticut, not far from the Franklin House Hotel where Mrs. Stratton sometimes worked.

Grandma Stratton, who lived with the family, and Charles's sisters, Frances Jane and Mary Elizabeth, were glad to help out with the new baby. It was fun to watch him learn about the world.

Charles started by burbling, as babies do. Then he reached for his yellow gourd rattle with the dry seeds inside. After a while he learned a kind of sideways crab crawl. Then he walked, like a tipsy little sailor just off a boat on nearby Long Island Sound.

Give him time, everyone thought. The little fellow would grow to match that top-heavy name, Charles Sherwood Stratton.

But as time went on, something came over the cottage on Dutch Lane, like a cloud over the sun. Frances Jane and Mary Elizabeth shot up like dandelions in a garden, but Charles had stopped growing. He was bright and clever and full of fun. Still, he hadn't grown an inch since he was five months old—and he was already past his fourth birthday.

People began to talk. Some whispered that a fairy must have kissed him in his cradle (though fairies had mostly gone out of fashion by 1838, when baby Charles was born).

One woman said, "Why that Stratton child isn't *half* as tall as my Josh." Another whispered, "It's a disgrace! Do you suppose his ma and pa feed that boy? I'd give him an eggnog every night at bedtime, if he were mine."

Another neighbor spoke right up to his ma. "That child needs more to eat. Like red flannel hash for supper. And a big bowl of porridge with maple sugar and thick cream for breakfast. Then he'd fatten up and begin to grow."

His sisters heard the talk and became ashamed, but Mrs. Stratton bristled. She gave the gossips a sharp piece of her mind. "He may be little," she told them angrily. "But he's as bright as a new penny. Your children can't hold a candle to my Charles. Why, he's only four, but he can read his letters from the *New England Primer*. All the way up to 'M' where it says, 'the Moon Gives light in time of Night.' That's more than most boys can do, *even big ones*. Besides, he can sing 'Yankee Doodle,' *all eleven verses*."

This was certainly true. But, as Charles knew, none of his cleverness could help him win a footrace. It couldn't help him walk upstairs. He had to crawl. He flew into tantrums when other children teased him. And when they saw how he hated to be called "little," they teased him all the more.

Even his sisters tormented him. They made Charles be their "baby" when they played house. They put doll dresses and baby bonnets on him, no matter how hard he fought. All this hurt his dignity.

So his parents sent for Dr. Nash. First the doctor wiggled his beard to make Charles laugh. Then he punched him gently in the stomach. He tapped his chest and listened to his heart. He looked at his tongue and said, "Say *ah*," as doctors have done since time began. Then he measured Charles and weighed him.

At last Dr. Nash nodded wisely and said, "This little fellow is as sound as a bell. There's nothing whatever wrong with him. Some children don't grow as fast as others. Just feed him well and love him."

So his ma and pa did. Charles was easy to love. He was a little mimic, as good as a catbird and full of tricks. He liked to hide in the basket on his ma's arm when she went to work at the hotel or under cabbages and apples when she went to market. Neighbors would stop to pass the time of day with her, and up Charles would pop, delighted by the surprise on their faces.

Yes, most of the time he was cheerful and full of fun.

But Charles hated being lifted up like a baby to sit at the table. Even when perched on cushions piled atop the thick family Bible, his chin was almost in his plate. And his legs went to sleep, all prickly the way legs get when they dangle.

So his family tried to make things easier for the tiny boy. His pa made Charles a little table and chair all his own. He cobbled boots, three inches long, from scraps of leather. His ma sewed little shirts from flour sacks and made him homespun britches. His grandma knitted tiny red mittens for winter. A kind neighbor took an interest in the boy. She stitched him a blue velvet suit with tiny buttons.

Mr. Stratton built a ladder for him to climb into bed.

News about the little boy who didn't grow traveled up and down the turnpike. The people of Bridgeport began to be proud of their amazing "midget," as they called him. They bragged about him to strangers.

Of course, nobody knew that Charles Sherwood Stratton's life would soon be like a fairy tale come true and that he'd travel to palaces and talk with queens and presidents. But that's just what happened.

One day Mr. Phineas Taylor Barnum, the showman from New York, came to Bridgeport. He had come to visit his half-brother, Philo, who owned the Franklin House Hotel.

"I've a surprise up my sleeve for you, P.T.," Philo told him. "It's a midget boy no bigger than a minute. I'll wager you'll want the lad for your American Museum."

"Let me see him!" Phineas Barnum said eagerly. "Though I don't guarantee I'll want to exhibit him. Midgets sometimes take a spurt of growing, remember."

So Philo sent word to Charles's ma. She dressed her tiny son in his new blue velvet suit.

"Don't carry me, please," he said. So holding his ma's hand, Charles walked proudly along to the hotel. He loved to wear that suit!

No one knows what he thought about meeting the famous Mr. Barnum, but that gentleman's eyes almost popped out of his head when he saw the boy. "You're four years old! Why, you look more like two. Can you talk, child?"

The Strattons lived in this cottage when Charles was born.
COURTESY, BARNUM MUSEUM

For the first and only time in his life, Charles was shy. Perhaps the tall gentleman with the excited face and the booming voice frightened him. Perhaps it was the new blue velvet suit. Whatever the reason, Charles said not one word.

"May I pay you a visit tomorrow, madame?" Phineas Barnum asked Mrs. Stratton. "Perhaps the child will find his tongue by then."

"Certainly, sir," Charles's ma replied. "I

can't think what's wrong with the boy. He's usually as full of words and mischief as the day is long."

So the next morning Phineas Barnum knocked at the door on Dutch Lane. When it opened, he doffed his tall beaver hat and bowed low.

"Madame Stratton," he said, just as if she were a grand lady. Charles's mother wiped her floury hands on her apron, for she was in the middle of making bread.

"Come in, sir," she said. "My husband, Sherwood, and I have been expecting you." She introduced Charles's pa to the visitor. Naturally Barnum settled himself in the best chair by the fire. The Strattons sat on three-legged stools, which Mr. Stratton had made.

"I've been asking folks about this tiny boy of yours," Barnum told them. "They say he just plain refuses to grow like other boys. Everybody seems to think he's a little marvel. I like marvels. Perhaps he belongs in my show at the American Museum in New York. That is, if he's as bright as he is pretty."

At these words Charles popped out from behind the cupboard door where he had been hiding. Suddenly he was a regular show-off. Without so much as a "How-d'-you-do," he began to sing "Yankee Doodle" in a voice like a meadowlark's. With his grandma's knitting needle stuck in his belt for a tiny sword, the child marched round and round the room. He sang every verse!

Phineas Barnum's face began to glow, his eyes to sparkle. He took Charles on his lap. "Why, I have just the name for you, my boy," he said. "Hereafter you shall be called 'Tom Thumb,' like the elf in the fairy tale."

Then and there he told Charles the story of the elfin Tom Thumb, who was one of King Arthur's Knights of the Round Table. Because he was little, he could do all sorts of things that other knights could never even dream of doing. He could swing through the air on a spider's thread and ride a white mouse for a steed. He could float on a pond with an oak leaf for a boat and a satin moth for a sail. Mr. Barnum was spellbinding. . . .

Charles was enchanted. He clapped his hands in delight.

"I like my new name," he crowed. "Tom Thumb! No other boy in all the world has such a fine name as mine."

His ma and pa were not so sure.

"Now, Tom," Phineas Barnum said, "I'd like you to go to New York with me. My American Museum there is the wonder of the world. Folks all over the land are talking about its marvels."

"What's a 'marvel'?" asked the new Tom Thumb.

"Well, there is a FeeJee mermaid: half woman, half fish. There's a tattooed man and a band of Indians from the Wild West. There are two giants, a juggler from Italy, acrobats from China, and a magnificent snake charmer. Now Tom Thumb will join my marvels. It isn't every day that people have a chance to see a real live midget."

Tom had been called a "midget" before, but now he was bold and asked, "What's a midget?" Then he looked steadily at the floor.

"Why, a midget is a fine young lad with bright eyes and pretty manners, just like yours," Barnum declared. He had a way of taking things in and coming up with just what the situation called for. He was quick with words and had a soft heart.

Charles perked up, so Barnum continued. "A midget is a boy whose body, just like yours, does not grow; *but his mind does.* He can learn to sing songs, tell a pretty yarn, dance a jig or two. . . ." Barnum had warmed to his subject. "A midget is a boy named Tom Thumb," he declared. "All the world will love you. Every man, lady, and child in the city of New York will be glad to pay their quarters to watch you do your clever act, which I will teach you."

Mrs. Stratton spoke up quickly at this.

"Why, he's only a little boy, sir. We couldn't let him leave us to go to New York with you!"

"Ah, Madame," the famous showman replied, "I am just coming to that. I hereby invite you to accompany your son at all times. I shall pay him three dollars a week, besides all expenses, while you and Tom Thumb are at my museum in New York."

So the Strattons talked the matter over. It seemed the offer of a lifetime. For Charles to join the American Museum was a chance to earn his living while still young. He would be able to build a nest egg for the uncertain years that lay ahead. So the boy's parents said "Yes" to Mr. Barnum.

His ma would go along to take care of her little son and teach him his three "R's." His grandma would stay home with Frances Jane, Mary Elizabeth, and Mr. Stratton. That man had never made much money himself, but he had a Yankee's good head for money matters. So he made Phineas Barnum put his plan in writing.

Charles was to be paid three dollars a week for four weeks—and more later if he deserved it. His new master meant to teach him dances and songs. He called them "acts." Tom Thumb would perform these acts for the stage show at the American Museum.

The Strattons were terribly proud. Their own son, Charles Sherwood Stratton, would soon be the toast of New York. Or so Mr. Barnum planned.

Before you could say "Tiddlywinks!" the new Tom Thumb rattled away down the turnpike in a stagecoach bound for New York. He was wearing his blue velvet suit and feeling quite puffed up. His ma was with him, of course. She held his little hand tightly. After all, the child was still not quite five years old.

CHAPTER

2

In New York, Tom and his ma rode in a horsecar pulled on a track. It was Thanksgiving Day, in the year 1842. Broadway was a sight to see. Store windows sparkled in the sun. Gentlemen in swallow-tailed coats and tall silk hats strolled up and down. Ladies lifted their long ruffled skirts daintily to cross the rough street. Carriages and gigs dashed up and down. A chestnut vendor hawked his wares on a tray hung round his neck. Here and there a pig trotted boldly down the sidewalk.

Their driver let Tom and his ma out in front of a huge building. The words "Barnum's American Museum" were painted in enormous letters across its front. There was also a wall poster as big as a bed sheet. It caught Mrs. Stratton's eye and made her mad as hops:

COME IN AND SEE
THE MARVELOUS MIDGET
TOM THUMB
ELEVEN YEARS OLD
AND NO BIGGER THAN A MINUTE
BROUGHT FROM ENGLAND AT GREAT EXPENSE
BY THE PRINCE OF SHOWMEN
PHINEAS T. BARNUM
ADMISSION: TWENTY-FIVE CENTS
CHILDREN HALF-PRICE

Dragging her son by the hand, Mrs. Stratton rushed into the museum. She burst into Mr. Barnum's office.

"How could you do such a thing?" she demanded. "My son is *not* eleven years old. He is *not quite five,* as you very well know. And he's *not from England* either!"

Mr. Barnum smoothed her ruffled feathers.

"Calm yourself, dear lady," he said gently. "My museum must entice people to pay good money to see its wonders. Sometimes I puff up my marvels just a bit to make folks curious.

Barnum's American Museum was an enormous building on Broadway, at Ann Street, in New York City.

"If I told them Tom is from Bridgeport, Connecticut, why he wouldn't seem special at all. And if I told them he is only four years old, they'd say, 'Why, he's not a real midget. He's just slow in growing.' In fact," he added, "who can be sure he won't take a spurt of growing any day? That would spoil everything! A midget who grows is no longer a midget."

Mrs. Stratton sat down quietly in a chair and took Tom on her lap. "There is some truth in what you say, sir, though not much."

"It's just a bit of hokum," Barnum said. "Folks call me the 'Prince of Humbug.' They don't seem to mind being spoofed if they like what I show them. But there must always be a grain of truth at the heart of the humbug."

He picked Tom up and tossed him high in the air.

"Come, my boy. We must get to work. If you're as bright as I think you are, you will learn to entertain everybody—country yokels and city folks alike—in a way to please them all."

From that minute Mr. Barnum became Tom's teacher. He taught the child songs and dances. He told Tom stories by the hour. He played marbles on the floor with him and, best of all, laughed at Tom's jokes. In fact, the flamboyant showman became Tom's best friend.

Barnum understood that it must be hard to be little in a world of people who looked like giants. He often glanced into the glass of his office door to admire his own reflection. Barnum was glad to be one of the giants, but he tried to make sure that Tom was happy.

He meant to make the boy—and himself—rich. They struck a new bargain. Barnum was never to call Tom "little" again. He promised always to say "diminutive" instead.

For days and days Tom and Barnum worked on new songs and marching steps. Tom even began to try a new dance, the "Pigeon Wing." Phineas had never seen so clever a child, or one more full of mischief. Tom liked nothing more than to tease. His favorite trick was to run around under a desk or table and pinch people's legs.

Now and then Tom had time to wander around the museum and see the exhibits. Some, like the FeeJee mermaid, were displayed in little rooms, in glass cases. Others, like the tattooed man and the snake charmer, were in the Hall of Living Curiosities.

Every afternoon at half-past two there was a grand show on the stage, where Tom would soon appear.

To his surprise, Tom discovered that the Chinese acrobats were not really Chinese. They came from Philadelphia. Before their act the five young men pasted skullcaps on their heads, each with a long black braid dangling behind. They also rubbed clay-colored paste on their faces and painted their eyes. The magician was a friendly man, who showed Tom the false bottom in his silk hat. Under this he kept a white rabbit with pink ears.

Tom told Barnum what he had discovered.

"It's all just a bit of that hokum I told you about," Phineas shrugged. "But those fellows are really fine acrobats, and the magician is a clever trickster. See that you learn to do as well."

At last Tom's act was ready. To begin, he was to sing his favorite, "Yankee Doodle."

Barnum took pains to explain that the song was really about an American soldier in the Revolutionary War. He gave Tom a wooden sword no bigger than a letter opener and taught him to brandish it with a fine flourish as he marched up and down the stage. He made sure that Tom learned to make the ladies' hearts flutter by throwing kisses to the audience during the applause.

Then it was time for a surprise, guaranteed—Barnum felt sure—to turn the boy into a true showman.

Half an hour before show time, a messenger knocked on Tom's door. He was holding a large box tied with a red, white, and blue ribbon. Tom tore it open. Inside he found a general's full uniform, made just to fit! There was a tall hat with a cockade, and gold medals decorated each shoulder of the red tunic. Best of all, there was a toy sword that looked for all the world like a real one.

Tom shouted with delight.

When he marched onstage to the music of fife and drum, Barnum went with him. The showman was six feet two inches tall; Tom was two feet plus a fraction of an inch tall. They made quite a pair.

The room was packed with gawking people. So this was the marvel which posters all up and down Broadway had promised them: a tiny child, no bigger than a minute. What new brand of hokum was this?

"Ladies and gentlemen!" P.T. Barnum's grand voice boomed. "I wish to introduce you, the patrons of my American Museum, to our latest marvel. I give you the diminutive General Tom Thumb himself! He is the smallest military genius in all the world. Today he will sing your favorite song, the favorite song of all America: 'Yankee Doodle!' "

Phineas swept off his tall hat and bowed with a flourish; first to the audience, then to Tom. With the bow there was also a wink and a whisper, "Go to it, my boy! Win their hearts!" For one second Phineas wondered if he had made a mistake. Suppose the child had an attack of stage fright? That would mean the end of all his golden plans.

He needn't have worried. Tom was as cool as a cucumber. Like the miniature general he seemed to be, Tom Thumb marched and swaggered and sang in a clear, true voice. He sang nine verses, plus the last two as an encore.

At once the audience loved the tiny general. Phineas Barnum had called him "The Smallest Military Genius in All the World." Was he real? Was Tom Thumb the boy he seemed to be? Was he really a tiny man in disguise? Who could tell? Phineas Barnum, they knew, was the Prince of Humbug. But they fell completely in love with General Tom Thumb. To prove it, they whistled and stamped their feet. They clapped until their hands hurt.

Offstage, Phineas swept Tom into his arms. He gave him a great bear hug and a new penny whistle.

"You did it! I knew you would! Now there's nothing you and I can't do, my boy—if we've a mind to. We'll make our fortunes. The golden rain has begun to fall!"

Tom looked a bit smug. Phineas thought he had a right to be proud. Being praised and applauded must be heady stuff for a not-quite five-year-old. It was still heady stuff for Barnum!

Country folk came to the city early to sell fresh vegetables and fruits. They wanted to see Tom before the markets opened, so the doors of the American Museum were opened at sunrise. In a very short time all of New York was asking, "Have you seen Tom Thumb?"

Nobody had ever seen anything like the "Marvelous Midget."

On the stage Tom danced the "Scottish Hornpipe," wearing a plaid kilt. He sang popular songs in a sweet, piping voice. He recited long poems. He told jokes. He posed with bow and arrow as a statue of Cupid, wearing pink tights and little wax wings. Sometimes he was a miniature Samson, the "strongest man who ever lived."

Best of all, he liked playing the part of the hero in the fairy tale "Jack and the Beanstalk." The giant was an enormous fellow, eight feet tall. Barnum had found him down at the docks loading ships and hired him on the spot. In the play the huge fellow was slain with one blow by the sword of Tom Thumb, the midget. This act was a roaring favorite with the crowds. After the show, they packed the Hall of Living Curiosities to meet the real Tom Thumb.

Newspapers began writing about Tom, too. One editor laughed at what he had heard about the tiny fellow.

"Don't be hoodwinked," he told his readers. "Our Prince of Humbug is full of tricks. This 'General Tom Thumb' is his newest spoof to take your good money."

So Phineas T. Barnum and General Tom Thumb paid a surprise visit to the gentleman's home one Sunday at dinner time. Without so much as a "By your leave," Phineas stood the child on the table. There Tom walked carefully among the plates and serving dishes. He bowed and shook hands politely with each member of the editor's family. Then he did a little hopping dance around the platter of roast beef.

He also ate a big plateful of that roast beef, when it was served to him later. "I may be small," Tom said, "but I have a grown-up appetite." (Which, indeed, he would always have.)

The next day the editor printed large headlines on the front page of his newspaper:

TOM THUMB NO HOAX— LITTLE GENERAL REAL

Tom soon lost count of how many pretty ladies swept him up into their arms and smothered him with kisses. Their furs and feathers tickled his face. Being kissed was a great bother, and he complained until Mr. Barnum decided to charge a dime for each kiss. Soon it cost another dime for the midget's name, written on a calling card just this size:

Gen. Tom Thumb

One "Lady Admirer" wrote a poem in his honor. After many verses, it ended with these words:

> *From Lilliput you must have come,*
> *You great, great wonder, little Thumb.*
> *May all your cares be little too,*
> *And so, dear little man, adieu.*

The museum became uncomfortably crowded. After customers had paid their quarters and seen the day's show, after they had gawked at the menagerie (a family of monkeys, a giraffe, and a zebra), after they had seen the FeeJee mermaid, the sword swallower, and the Tom Thumb Show, Mr. Barnum expected them to leave. Instead, whole families pulled lunches from their pockets and settled down to see the exhibits and watch the show a second time.

There wasn't room inside for people waiting to pay their quarters at the door!

Phineas looked up his sleeve and, as usual, found a trick in it.

"Keep a close eye, Tom," he said with a twinkle. "I'll show you that what I've often said is true: A fool is born every minute."

So Barnum hung a large sign over the "Exit"
door of the museum. "TO THE EGRESS!" it
read. He and Tom watched from a dark corner.
Few people understood the new word. Who
could tell? Perhaps the "egress" was a new wild
animal from Africa. Perhaps it was a newfan-
gled invention.

Not wishing to miss a thing, most people
walked through the door. To their dismay, they
found themselves in the street outside! It would
take more of their precious quarters to get back
into the museum.

When he learned that "egress" meant "exit,"
Tom laughed until tears rolled down his cheeks.
Like Barnum, his teacher, Tom loved money,
puns, and impressive words. He knew why people called his friend the Prince of Ballyhoo!

Phineas watched the boy closely. He knew
that Tom had no friends his own age and size.
And it must give the child a crick in his neck
to have to look up into people's faces all the
time—except when he was onstage.

No five-year-old boy would like being patted
on the head a hundred times a day. Or being
dandled on the knees of strangers. Or being
kissed by ladies at every turn. The trouble was,

Tom Thumb seemed a "child" to grown-ups and a "little man" to other children. He didn't quite fit with anybody.

So Phineas did his best to be a true friend. To keep Tom from being lifted up like a baby, he gave him a tiny bed, a small red plush sofa, and a folding ladder to help him reach things. These went everywhere (the sofa even went to Buckingham Palace) with Tom.

At night, Barnum would read him bedtime stories. Tom liked these so much that Barnum got tired. He decided that Tom would have to pay a quarter from his own pocket money to hear the endings.

Tom did not like paying his own quarter to find out how Ali Baba escaped from the forty thieves. For years he was to be stingy about money, though the Stratton family was no longer poor. Tom was already earning seven dollars a week. Soon it would be much more. For Tom Thumb was now P.T. Barnum's prize exhibit at the American Museum.

Often the showman took his midget friend home to visit the Barnum family. Mrs. Charity Barnum was jolly and motherly. She and Cynthia Stratton became friends, too. Mrs. Barnum baked tiny mint pasties especially to please Tom and knitted him an elfin pair of red slippers.

But the Barnum girls spoiled it all. They begged Tom to play house with them and be their doll baby, just as Tom's sisters had done before he was famous. General Tom Thumb a doll baby? Phineas could understand why Tom was hurt at the very idea.

At five, he knew the simple *New England Primer* by heart, and he could easily read the sandwich boards worn by hired men as they walked up and down Broadway in front of the American Museum. These moving advertisements, in letters a foot high, asked, "HAVE YOU SEEN TOM THUMB?" and announced, "ONE OF THE WONDERS OF THE WORLD!" or "THE SMALLEST MAN IN ALL NEW YORK!—Admission 25¢."

One of Barnum's many posters advertising the appearance of General Tom Thumb.

COURTESY, HARVARD THEATRE COLLECTION

American
MUSEUM
AERIAL GARDEN, & FAIR.

Cor Broadway & Ann-st.　　P. T. Barnum, Manager

This Establishment embraces SIX SPACIOUS HALLS, each more than One Hundred Feet in length, and containing 500,000 Natural and Artificial Curiosities from every portion of the Globe.

☞ DAY VISITORS admitted the same Evening FREE. ☜

☞ *Every Day and Evening this Week* ☜
COMMENCING THURSDAY, OCT. 5, 1843.

☞ The Manager is happy to inform the public that in accordance with numerous and repeated requests, he has effected a short engagement with

GEN. TOM THUMB

The most SURPRISING and DELIGHTFUL CURIOSITY the world ever produced! He can be seen throughout the whole day and evening. The wonderful diminutiveness of the General, his beautiful proportions, graceful manners, sprightliness, wit, intelligence and good humor are so captivating that none fail to be delighted and almost charmed with him. Not to see him is to miss a sight of by far the MOST INTERESTING WONDER OF THE WORLD! With all the above qualifications, the General is still

The Smallest Person that ever Walked Alone!

He is 11 years Old, 25 Inches High, and

Weighs Only 15 Pounds.

The Manager has pleasure in announcing an engagement, for this week only, with

DR. VALENTINE !

The Celebrated Delineator of American Peculiarities, who will open his ENTIRE BUDGET of Bits, Scraps, Oddities, Whims, Rare Doings Diversions, &c

Also Engaged

MR. S. K. G. NELLIS

Who will display the *ASTONISHING POWERS* with which Nature has endowed him, in the

Use of his Feet and Toes !

He will cut profiles of any person present, Fold a Puzzle Letter, WRITE WITH HIS TOES! CUT A BEAUTIFUL WATCH PAPER! LOAD AND DISCHARGE A PISTOL! With a BOW & ARROW hit a quarter dollar held in the hand of any visitor! Play the Accordion and Violincello, and perform many other wonderful feats with his toes which

MUST BE SEEN TO BE BELIEVED!

The newspaper was also Tom's school book. Almost every morning now there was a headline about the "Diminutive General" or "New York's Darling—Our Midget Tom Thumb."

As a surprise Phineas had a miniature costume made for Tom. It exactly matched his own swallow-tailed coat, high beaver hat, and flowered waistcoat. Sometimes the two did a show together on the stage at the museum. Step, glide; step, glide; a bit of repartee; then a twirl and a flourish of their silver-topped walking canes. They left the stage with Tom Thumb sitting high on P.T. Barnum's shoulder. This act brought the house down—always—with clapping and whistling.

Phineas could see that Tom loved applause. In fact, the boy was stagestruck. The showman said nothing about it, but he was tickled pink. Tom might not enjoy being little, but there was not the least doubt that he liked being famous.

Money poured into their pockets. It quite took Phineas's breath away. There seemed no likely end to the "golden rain," for Tom grew too slowly for anyone to notice. But Phineas T.

Barnum was a restless man. Now that all New York loved General Tom Thumb, it was time to think of something new.

CHAPTER

3

Suddenly Barnum had an idea. Why not take Tom to England to visit the queen? That would make the world sit up and take notice. To understand why, you have to remember that it was 1843. America had just beaten England again, in the War of 1812. That's part of why "Yankee Doodle" was such a popular song! If an American general could win the heart of the English queen, it would give people something to talk about for years to come.

It was an outrageous idea. Royalty didn't speak to commoners in those days—and Barnum and Tom Thumb were in show business! Why, when the Beatles were knighted by Queen Elizabeth, more than 125 years later, people would think it a scandal!

Barnum flew into action, writing to the English newspapers, making arrangements, and trying to wangle an invitation to Buckingham Palace.

Tom's ma was asked to travel with her son. His pa went along to manage the money. A teacher was hired to give Tom lessons from proper school books (but Barnum would teach Tom all of the proper manners for visiting the queen—once he'd learned them himself).

They all arrived at the New York docks on a bright January day in 1844, ready to board the *Yorkshire* and sail for England. There had been much ballyhoo in the papers, of course, but even Barnum was surprised by the size of the crowd. Thousands of people lined the pier to wave farewell to their beloved Tom Thumb.

"Good-bye, Little General! We will miss you. Give our greetings to the queen!" they shouted. A brass band, hired by Barnum, struck up "Yankee Doodle." As a joke, and to please the people, Tom did his "Yankee Doodle" act right there on the ship's upper deck. Phineas was delighted. He could already see the headlines—on both sides of the Atlantic! But it wasn't that easy.

Though messages had been sent ahead, the docks were empty when they landed in England. To make matters worse, P.T. Barnum and General Tom Thumb hadn't been invited to Buckingham Palace.

Those English needed to see the Prince of Hokum in action!

So Barnum rented a handsome house on a fashionable street and paid a great deal of money for it. He felt perfectly sure that the "golden showers" would come just as soon as his general had the chance to visit the queen.

He sent invitations for teas and supper parties to the finest lords and ladies of the realm. These read:

PHINEAS TAYLOR BARNUM, ESQUIRE,

of New York, U.S.A.,

invites

Lord and Lady such-and-such

to high tea on Tuesday afternoon

at half after four o'clock

to meet

GENERAL TOM THUMB,

the toast of America.

Here was a new kind of party. The lords and ladies laughed. Still, they came out of curiosity. It might be amusing to see this crude American showman and his "general." To their own surprise they stayed to marvel. The pretty child was not only clever, he had fine manners. They went home to tell their children about tiny Tom Thumb.

Finally the queen's curiosity got the best of her. A shining coach drew up to Barnum's front door. Out stepped one of the queen's Life Guards in full dress. He had a message from the royal lady herself. It said:

Her Majesty, Victoria, Queen of England,
commands an audience with Mr. Phineas Taylor Barnum
and his General Tom Thumb
on the twenty-third of March,
at eight-thirty in the evening,
at Buckingham Palace.

When the door closed behind the footman, Phineas and Tom danced around the room. All of Barnum's plans had worked—the queen was curious.

39

The next few days were a flurry of preparations. Tom's court suit must be fitted and stitched. It was to be made of brown velvet and must have knee britches. There were to be silver buttons on the coat, silver buckles on the shoes, and a frill of lace under Tom's chin. He was also fitted with a powdered curly wig.

"American boys don't wear lace on their shirts!" Tom stormed. "They don't wear wigs either!"

"American boys don't often appear at the queen's court," Phineas replied.

There were more important things to worry about than lace under a boy's chin. Tom must learn a new dance and a long poem called *The Boy Stood on the Burning Deck.* It was all the rage back in America.

He had to learn to sing a new song, called "Blow, Bugle, Blow!" To top it off, Tom had to practice posing like a tiny Napoleon.

Phineas felt pretty sure Tom could do these acts well enough to delight any queen. But how about the child's manners? Could a six-year-old boy master a proper courtly bow? Would he learn how to leave the Queen's Royal Presence?

Barnum studied the rules for visiting the

queen, and then he drilled them with Tom.

You must bow at every fourth step. Coming and going.

Never turn your back upon the queen. That meant backing slowly out of the throne room with a deep bow at every fourth step.

Never begin a conversation with a queen. Would Tom remember not to speak unless first spoken to? After all, the child had been brought up in free and easy America, and he was a famous star to boot.

"When you address the queen for the first time, say 'Your Majesty and ladies and gentlemen of the court,' " Barnum repeated time and again.

It was most unlike the showman to worry about such formalities, and there was some comfort in the fact that Queen Victoria had sent word that she wished "to see the little general in his natural state."

Still, Barnum had never before appeared in the queen of England's throne room. He himself had been born a simple Yankee boy. Now he wondered if his own manners would be polished enough for Buckingham Palace.

Tom knew that Queen Victoria had two children, and he was excited by the prospect of meeting them. He imagined that a prince would be too noble to laugh at a midget or tease him for being small. It was Tom's great hope to find a friend at the palace.

At last it was the twenty-third and the hours ticked by. Phineas pulled his snow-white gloves off and on, nervously waiting for the royal coach. When it came, pulled by four white horses, Tom was as cool as a spring morning. He twirled his tiny cane with the silver knob and looked out the windows as the coach traveled through the darkening streets of London.

They cantered through the gates of Buckingham Palace, passing the royal guards in their scarlet coats and high fur hats. Then they stopped at the palace itself.

A lord-in-waiting opened the door to the coach with a flourish. With great ceremony, P.T. Barnum and the general were announced to the queen of England.

Huge carved doors swung open. Tom gasped and shivered a bit. By now Phineas had grown calm, as he always did before appearing on stage. He put his steady hand for a moment on Tom's shoulder and said, "Easy does it, lad. Just remember your manners: they're the manners of a fine American boy."

The floor of the throne room looked like a lake of shimmering water, its marble shone so. At its end was a high throne. On the throne, not wearing a crown at all, sat a little lady dressed plainly. She looked for all the world like someone's mother, which she was. She held a small white poodle on her lap. The lords and ladies surrounding her were far more elegant!

Tom and Phineas approached Queen Victoria's throne. They had practiced for days just how to do this. Still, Phineas knew it was hard for Tom's short legs to match his own long strides. At every fourth step, the two Americans paused and bowed from the waist in the proper way.

At last they reached the throne, where they bowed low again.

The queen spoke first, as was the rule. "Sirs," she said, "you may entertain us."

It was time for Tom to recite his poem and do a bit of dancing. To begin with, he completely forgot to say the proper words. Instead, the six-year-old boy gave the greeting he always

used in his act at the American Museum.

"Good evening, ladies and gentlemen," Tom said grandly. Phineas gasped and so did the lords and ladies, but the queen did not look shocked. She waved her hand for him to continue.

Phineas held his breath while Tom recited his poem, sang the bugle song, and danced the "Victoria Slide." It had been Barnum's idea to give the queen's own name to the dance.

As he knew they would, the English loved the sight of Tom posing as a miniature French Napoleon.

When the act was over, there was a polite patter of applause. Tom beamed, and Phineas found that he could breathe again. The queen looked pleased. She took Tom by the hand and led the child around the great room.

"What do you think of all these pictures, my little man?" she asked him.

Fifty-five years after meeting Tom Thumb, Victoria was still queen of England —and she still dressed plainly.
COURTESY, NATIONAL PORTRAIT GALLERY

"Why, I think they're first rate, ma'am," he said cheerfully. "Only I thought you had some children to show me. Where are they?"

"The little prince and princess are in bed at this hour, where you should also be," Queen Victoria told Tom. "You shall come again and meet them at tea another day."

Then it was time to leave. The queen surprised everyone by bending to kiss General Tom Thumb good-bye. No one had ever heard of such a thing. There was a murmur as the queen sat back on her throne, taking her poodle back on her lap.

This time Tom remembered his lessons in courtly manners. Still, backing his way over that shining floor was not easy. It felt like slippery ice under his feet. At every fourth step, Tom took a quick look behind him at Phineas. His tall friend's long legs stepped three times farther than his own short ones. Tom was horrified to see that Barnum would reach the door of the throne room long before he did.

The thought of being the only American left in Buckingham Palace, even for a minute, made Tom's head swim. He forgot the command, "*Never* turn your back upon a queen!"

Instead, Tom backed three more steps, made his bow, then turned and *ran* as fast as his little legs would carry him, to catch up with Mr. Barnum.

He turned again to face the queen. "Step, step, step, bow—then *turn and run like mad!*" he told himself. "Step, step, step, bow—then *turn and run like mad!*"

Suddenly Tom realized that people were laughing—laughing at him—when he was being most polite and not trying to be funny at all! Just as suddenly the poodle jumped from the queen's lap. No one knows why. Perhaps the dog was jealous. Yapping loudly, it began nipping Tom's heels.

This was too much. A boy must protect himself from a nipping dog, even when that dog belongs to a queen. So Tom began hitting the creature with his cane.

"Stop him! Stop him!" someone shouted. Did that mean stop Tom Thumb or stop the dog? No one knew, but in a thrice, a lord-in-waiting swooped down on the furious pet. The poodle was taken back to Her Majesty's lap.

Tom's last glimpse of the royal court of England caught the queen and her lords and ladies laughing merrily—at him! Tom's pride was hurt and he was angry.

Of course the newspapers of London wrote stories about that court visit. "Queen Pleased with Tiny American General!" the headlines screamed on every street corner. "Queen's Dog Jealous of Miniature Man," said another. Tom blushed to see them. For three days Phineas tried to tempt him outdoors, but Tom wouldn't go. He even gave Tom a beautiful little boat to sail on the lake in St. James's Park. At any other time, Tom would have loved sailing that boat, but now he wouldn't budge. Someone might laugh at him.

Phineas tried again to soothe Tom's feelings.

"Our visit to the queen went well, my boy. They won't forget you at the court of England. Mark my words."

He was right, as Barnum so often was. Next morning the royal coach again stopped at the Barnum door. This time the Life Guard brought a present from the queen herself to the "Little General." It was a sack of gold coins and another invitation to the palace. This time it was for high tea with the Prince of Wales, named "Bertie," and his sister, the Princess Royal, who was called "Pussy" by her family.

When he saw them, Tom was disappointed. He thought them "babies," for they were only about half his own age. They could talk of nothing but a new rocking horse and a doll that could nod its head.

To this visit Tom took his red plush sofa. He politely invited the little princess to sit beside him, which she did. He also measured himself beside the prince. Later he told Mr. Barnum, "The prince is taller than I am, but I feel as big as anybody."

Queen Victoria talked with the children while they took their tea. It was plain nursery food: bread and milk and treacle tarts. Tom had expected something much finer.

"Do you draw, my little man?" the queen asked Tom.

"Yes, I frequently draw and can do it very well," he replied.

Queen Victoria did not know that Tom and Barnum often played games with words. He was punning. Tom always "drew" crowds to see him sing and dance.

Next morning another present arrived at the Barnum house. It was a fine mahogany and silver box filled with artists' pencils and brushes. With it there was a note in the queen's own handwriting. It said, "So that some of the tiny general's art may be framed and hung on the wall for all to see."

Tom and Phineas laughed at the "drawing" joke. Secretly Tom had hoped for a pony, but he sent the queen a message, saying "I am very much obliged and will keep this present as long as I live."

"That's the spirit," Phineas declared. "It's time we rented a hall—a big one—and began showing you to all the people. They'll batter down the door to see the diminutive Tom Thumb—the American general who has charmed their queen. We've found the pot of gold at the foot of the rainbow, Tom, or I miss my guess."

Then P.T. Barnum hired a large hall where he and Tom played all their old acts and several new ones. People came in droves. They were as happy to pay their English shillings as New Yorkers had been to part with their quarters. Overnight Tom Thumb became the pet of London. Money poured in. Sometimes Mr. Stratton had to hire a special cab to take the heavy money bags to the bank.

Phineas and Tom were fast becoming rich.

The city became "Tom Thumb crazy." There were soon Tom Thumb paper dolls in toy-shop windows. A new sweet, called "Tom Thumb Sugar Plums," was sold on the street. Miniature milk jugs shaped like the little general appeared on shop shelves. Dancing masters began teaching a new step called the "Tom Thumb Polka." One day Tom saw a puppet show about himself. It was being shown to English children in Kensington Garden. Suddenly his own life seemed a fairy tale, which, in a way, it was.

It was like this everywhere they went in Europe. In France he was hailed as *Le Petit Pouce*, which meant "Little Thumb." He had a quick ear for language and starred in a play, *Le Petit Pouce*, which had been written expressly for him—in French. He was feted by the king, who raced toy sailboats with him on the lake in the Tuileries Palace garden. He watched bullfights in Spain from a royal perch—on the young Queen Isabella's lap.

No wonder Tom began to feel, as his pa said, "Too big for his britches."

Phineas glowed with pride. "I am the goose, my boy, and you are my golden egg!"

Tom had been showered with presents at every turn. One of the best was a surprise designed by Barnum. It was a miniature Cinderella coach, all red, white, and blue. On its doors were the American eagle and the British lion. In large letters were the words "GO AHEAD!"

Four matched Shetland ponies pulled the tiny coach through the streets and countryside. On its roof sat two seven-year-old boys, small for their age, but not midgets. One was coachman, the other footman. They wore cocked hats, curly powdered wigs, and sky-blue coats with red knee britches. Wigs on other boys especially delighted Tom, and, for a time, the boys were friendly to their midget master.

Sometimes they would travel by stagecoach, while Tom's tiny coach rode along in a van. But whenever Tom whirled along the roads in his little carriage, people dashed out of their doors to see the astonishing sight.

"Is the tiny boy a prince?" asked one man.

With his tongue in his cheek, P.T. Barnum replied. "Yes, indeed. He's Prince Charles the First, of the dukedom of Bridgeport, in the kingdom of Connecticut."

The man bowed deeply, then ran to tell his friends of the marvel, unaware that he'd just been talking to the Prince of Hokum.

By the time Barnum was known as "The Greatest Showman on Earth," Tom's coachman and footman had outgrown their uniforms. They began to look a bit ridiculous perched atop the tiny coach. Other small boys took their places. Then there were others. It did precious little good to keep hiring new small friends for Tom. They could not be kept from growing. By now the general was eight years old, though the public thought he was fifteen. Posters had begun calling him "The Twenty-five-Inch Man!" He had grown a little, though scarcely enough to notice. Tom Thumb would be a midget all his life.

Tom and Phineas began to feel a little homesick. It was time to return to America.

CHAPTER
4

When their ship landed in New York, thousands of people waited on the dock. They waved flags and shouted, "Tom Thumb! Our Tom Thumb!" Barnum and his little general were by now very rich indeed. As partners, they divided their money equally, and Sherwood Stratton had managed it well during the European tour.

Some folks whispered that the tall man and the tiny boy were millionaires when they returned from abroad. In fact, later Phineas wrote a book which he called *How I Made Millions.*

The first thing Tom did with his money was to build a fine home for the Stratton family in Bridgeport, where folks still called him "Our little Charlie." It was three stories high and had a cupola on top. From it a watcher, even without a telescope, could see boats coming and

The grand house Tom built for his family.
COURTESY, BARNUM MUSEUM

going on Long Island Sound. Tom had always loved boats.

In the fine new house there was plenty of room for Tom's sisters, who no longer teased him about being small. Later there would be a

57

new baby brother, William, who would grow to a normal height.

Attached to the house was a special apartment of Tom's very own. The doorways were low. Nobody but a small child or a midget could walk through them. The rooms were also just the right size, with windows low enough for Tom to see out without standing on tiptoe.

Furniture was mostly beautiful gifts which the little general had been given during his travels abroad. A cozy chair and footstool were pulled up near the fireplace. There Tom could sit and toast himself in front of his own bright fire on a winter night. He drank hot chocolate from tiny cups lined with gold. (These were not much bigger than doll dishes.) And, settled by the fire, he could enjoy miniature books only two inches square, which told his own story. Children everywhere were reading these.

When sleepy, Tom tucked himself into a rosewood bed with fine carvings. This was a present from the French Court. It was four feet long. A patchwork quilt, made from scraps of silk, covered him cozily from head to toe.

Phineas was also in a building mood. His house, which he named "Iranistan," was like a

Tom's rosewood bed can be seen at the Barnum Museum.
COURTESY, BARNUM MUSEUM

Persian palace. The name meant "eastern country place" or "oriental villa." It had turrets and towers, arches and balconies. Reindeer and elk ran freely in a grassy park. Gardens were filled with roses and singing fountains. People came from miles around to gawk at it. Inside, the Barnums gave great parties for a thousand guests at a time.

Barnum's Iranistan was a sight to behold.

The train track from New Haven to New York crossed the edge of Phineas Barnum's lawn. Just in case its passengers did not stare curiously enough at his startling new home, Phineas dreamed up a new stunt. He bought an elephant which he hooked to a plow. The plowman was dressed in an Arabian costume, with turban and billowing trousers. Four times a day, just at train time, the elephant and its driver plowed the lawn in front of Iranistan.

Still, Barnum and Tom Thumb grew restless. It seemed time for more excitement. Besides, all of America was clamoring to see its darling general.

Up and down the United States they went. They journeyed by stagecoach on dusty or muddy turnpikes, by steamboat on rivers and canals. Sometimes they rode on the amazing new steam train, then called the "Teakettle-on-a-track." Often Tom's own little coach and ponies went with them. These delighted thousands of cheering people.

Tom had long ago lost track of how many gentlemen had patted him on the head, calling him "My little man." As for ladies, Tom wrote a letter to an admirer, who asked for his autograph:

Congress Hall   Albany July 22d /47

Respected Sir

In accordance with your request, I send you a little note. My travels have thus far been chiefly in England Scotland Ireland France, Belgium Spain and a portion of the United States.

I was born in Bridgeport Ct the 11 of January 1832. I have travelled fifty thousand miles been before more crowned heads than any other yankee living, except my friend Mr Barnum, and have kissed nearly Two Millions of ladies including the Queens of England France, Belgium and Spain.

I read the Bible every day and am very fond of reading the New Testament. I love my Saviour and it makes me happy, I adore my Creator and know that He is good to us all. He has given me a small body but I believe he has not contracted my heart, nor brain, nor soul. I shall praise His name evermore.

Time compels me to make this note short like myself.

I am my dear sir Truly Yours

Charles S Stratton
known as
General Tom Thumb

To Reu Dr Sprague
Albany

Tom estimated that he'd kissed "nearly two millions of ladies, including the queens of England, France, Belgium and Spain." (When he wrote this, Tom was really nine years old. He always used Barnum's figure for his birthdate.)

COURTESY, HARVARD THEATRE COLLECTION

After this trip there were others. Sometimes Phineas stayed in Iranistan with his family. Sometimes Tom's father went with him on tours across America. As he grew older, Tom sometimes traveled with a manager or alone. He visited President Polk and the First Lady at the White House in Washington. Once he sailed to Cuba to give a show.

Phineas Barnum was still bursting with new notions. His American Museum wasn't enough to keep him busy, so he dreamed up a traveling show. He called it *Barnum's Great Asiatic Caravan, Museum, and Menagerie* and sent halfway around the world to Ceylon for a shipload of elephants. Wild animals in cages, acrobats, and ladies on high tightropes began touring the country, giving their show under canvas tents.

This was the first large American circus. Wild excitement greeted it in cities and small towns across America. Men went ahead of the show to paste enormous red and yellow posters on the sides of barns and fences: "Barnum's circus is coming to town!"

People hurried to spread the news. Circus Day became the high point of the year for grown-ups and children, too.

For several years Tom went with the show as its prize "general." Seeing him delighted everybody. But more and more often he stayed home in the pretty apartment which was his very own.

Like everyone else, Tom Thumb was getting older by the minute. He had grown slowly and only a little. On his nineteenth birthday, Barnum announced his true age to the world, which thought him to be twenty-six years old.

While grown-up in birthdays, he was still only the size of most four-year-old boys, though he was starting to get plump. He weighed twenty-nine pounds and was only thirty-one inches tall. He could still walk under a table without dipping his head. But he was grown-up and no longer pinched people's legs.

In fact, Tom Thumb was a dashing young gentleman who walked with a swagger, twirling his favorite cane. He had elegant manners and an uncommon education.

Besides all this, Tom was immensely rich. He began entertaining himself, buying fine ponies and sleek horses to enter in races. He bought sailing boats of normal size, then hired sailors to race these for him on Long Island Sound.

Once his sailboat, the *Maggie B.*, won an important race against many other fine yachts. The prize was a huge silver punch bowl.

"That bowl is plenty big enough for you to take a bath in!" someone said. Tom laughed at the teasing. He was proud of that prize and kept it all his life. It sat on his mother's sideboard. His own, of course, was too little to hold it.

In all the excitement, Barnum's Good Luck Fairy suddenly seemed to forget him.

It was really Barnum's generous heart that began the trouble. To help friends in Bridgeport, the showman had lent a large sum of money to the Jerome Clock Company. Alas, the company failed! To the world's astonishment and Phineas's dismay, he lost every penny. One newspaper said he'd lost half-a-million dollars. Phineas Taylor Barnum a poor man? It was almost impossible to believe.

For a while Phineas was like a balloon that has been pricked. He did not know how to begin again, for he was no longer a young man with fresh dreams and energy.

One day he received a letter from Tom, sent from the Jones Hotel in Philadelphia, the city where Tom was touring:

*My dear Mr. Barnum—I understand your friends, and that
means "all creation," intend to get up some benefits for your
family. Now, my dear sir, just be good enough to remember
that I belong to that mighty crowd, and I must have a finger
(or at least a "thumb") in that pie. I am bound to appear on
all such occasions in some shape, from "Jack the Giant
Killer," upstairs, to the doorkeeper, down, whichever may
serve you best; and there are some feats that I can perform as
well as any other man of my inches. I have just started out
on my western tour, and have my carriage, ponies, and
assistants all here, but I am ready to go on to New York, bag
and baggage, and remain at Mrs. Barnum's service as long as
I, in my small way, can be useful. Put me into "heavy"
work, if you like. Perhaps I cannot lift as much as some
other folks, but just take your pencil in hand and you will see
I can draw a tremendous load. I drew two hundred tons at a
single pull to-day, embracing two thousand persons, whom I
hauled up safely and satisfactorily to all parties, at one
exhibition. Hoping that you will be able to fix up a lot of
magnets that will attract all New York, and volunteering to
sit on any part of the loadstone, I am, as ever, your little but
sympathizing friend,*

Gen. Tom Thumb.

Tom did more than offer him money. He
helped Barnum make a fresh beginning with his
show business. They went again to England.

Queen Victoria still remembered her American general. He was invited again to the palace. In fact, all of England remembered Tom

66

Thumb. People crowded the halls where Tom sang and joked and danced, as winning as ever. Many children were seeing him for the first time.

But just as things seemed to be going well again, there was a fire. Iranistan burned. People were shocked. One newspaper headline called it "THE FALL OF BARNUM!"

People had long ago seen through Barnum's ballyhoo. But the showman had been right when he told Tom years earlier, "Everybody loves a bit of humbug." They also loved Phineas T. Barnum for himself. Old and young admired his bouncing spirit and open nature. Again and again folks said, "That Barnum is a rascal, but he's a jolly good fellow."

So everyone agreed with the newspaper which wrote, "Phineas Barnum's museum has been a fountain of delight to the children of New York. We grieve with Mr. Barnum in his loss."

In all, there were five fires in the showman's life before his spell of bad luck ran out. One was a fire in the tent of his traveling circus. Two times the American Museum burned. No lives were ever lost, but each time Phineas had to work like a wren to rebuild his fortune. Rebuild it he did, five times. Again and again, Tom proved his loyalty to Barnum.

As for the little general, he had everything in the world a young man's heart could wish for—race horses, a beautiful sailing yacht, and a gold watch with a chain and a key for winding it. In most ways he was happy. But, as he told Phineas one day, "In my pretty home I am more alone than ever before. I cannot even ask you, my oldest and best friend, to eat with me at my own table."

Phineas laughed. "I would be as awkward as a bull in a china shop, trying to eat from your tiny dishes. Besides, how could I squeeze through your tiny door?" Both of them laughed at the thought.

Still, being lonely is no laughing matter. Tom was tired of having a crick in his neck from looking up into people's faces. He longed for a friend exactly his size to share his life—a friend who would not outgrow him.

Tom struck out on his own again, touring the Midwest.

There was a wistful look on his face these days when he sang one of his favorite songs:

I should like to marry, if I could only find
Any pretty lady, suited to my mind.
I should like her handsome—I should like her good,
With a little money; yes, indeed I should.
Oh! then I would marry, if I could only find
A very pretty lady, suited to my mind.

When Tom sang this, young ladies' hearts fluttered. They fluttered even more when Tom Thumb, the toast of America, bowed and kissed their hands. Ladies no longer dared to pick him up and smother him with kisses. That would have been undignified for a tiny gentleman who was so romantic, famous, and rich. If only he had not been quite so small, it would have been easy for even the prettiest lady to fall in love with General Tom Thumb.

Tom continued his touring so Phineas hired a new midget for his American Museum, one Commodore Nutt. He began trying to turn the commodore into a great success.

CHAPTER
5

Then Barnum met a young lady as pretty as a princess. Her round face was dimpled; her black eyes merry. The first sight of her set his thinking cap awhirl. What wonderful luck! The lady herself was a midget.

She was also dainty, clever, and sweet. Her education and manners were as fine as Tom's own. Her name seemed longer than she was tall: Mercy Lavinia Warren Bump. She had been a teacher of third-grade children, all bigger than she.

Barnum hired her on the spot, along with her younger midget sister, Minnie.

For a time it looked as if Lavinia would succumb to the attentions of Commodore Nutt, but Barnum decided to play Cupid and see what might happen. Next to a bit of spoofing, nothing in the world delighted Phineas T. Barnum as much as a surprise.

So he sent Tom an invitation to visit the Barnums at their new home, built since Iranistan burned. There was no ballyhoo about Lavinia Warren. Meeting that pretty lady quite took Tom's breath away. Almost at once he called her "Vinnie."

The two young people went riding in Tom's carriage. They picnicked under apple trees. They watched the moon rise on a summer night, sweet with honeysuckle. They walked in a garden full of roses. Tom took Vinnie sailing on his new steam yacht. Vinnie baked Tom a coconut cake for his birthday. They visited Tom's house with its tiny apartment built for "Little People," as Vinnie called midgets. Very soon they found that they liked the same things, especially each other.

Tom had never really expected to fall in love, but that is exactly what he did. In no time at all, he asked Lavinia, "Will you marry me?" And Mercy Lavinia Warren Bump kissed him and said, "Yes."

It had been dreadfully hard for Phineas to wait patiently for this piece of news. When the lovers told him their plans, Barnum rubbed his hands together with glee. General Tom Thumb had proved that *one* midget was a gold mine. Think of the fame and fortune *two* such rare and pretty little people would mean to his show. Why, the whole world would be afire to see them—with not a whit of humbug needed, for Vinnie and Tom were real!

Tom and Lavinia were shocked. "Thank you kindly, sir," Vinnie told Mr. Barnum. Though her voice was soft, there was a firm light in her eyes. "Tom and I have enough money already. We also have each other. We will never again show ourselves on a stage or in a circus ring."

Phineas gave in with good grace. "Then you must let me give you a fine wedding," he said. "It will be a proper one, I promise you, for a bride and groom that the whole world will love."

"No tickets sold at the door," Tom said firmly. "Our wedding is *not* to be part of the 'Greatest Show on Earth.' "

Though dashed, Barnum promised: "It will be a beautiful wedding, fitting for Mr. Charles Sherwood Stratton and his lovely bride, Miss Mercy Lavinia Warren Bump."

So invitations were sent to two thousand wedding guests. Presents began to arrive in every mail. They were seven-day wonders. There was a tiny grand piano for Vinnie, who loved to play. There was a silver-plated sewing machine, which Vinnie used to make part of her trousseau and curtains and pillow covers for her new home.

Queen Victoria of England sent the bride an ermine cape. There were also tiny silver tea services and chocolate pots and a child-sized porcelain dinner set with the Tom Thumb monogram. There were rings and feather fans and tiny embroidered gloves for Vinnie. There were jeweled tiepins for the groom and candle-sticks, three inches tall, for the mantelpiece.

Mr. and Mrs. Phineas Taylor Barnum sent the bride and groom a charming Swiss music box. When it was wound, the golden bird on its spun-silver nest sang as sweetly as a nightingale.

On a snowy afternoon—February 10, 1863—Lavinia and Tom were married in Grace Church, in New York City. The bride's gown was made of satin and lace. It was trimmed with seed pearls and had a tiny train. There were fifty-two hoops inside the skirt. In her hair, Lavinia wore a diamond star, and other diamonds shone like

*The best man, Commodore Nutt, and
bridesmaid, Minnie Bump, stand on
either side of the newlyweds.*

dewdrops around her pretty neck. She was a
"Fairy Bride" indeed.

Tom was dignified and handsome in a fine
new swallow-tailed coat. His gold watch chain
was draped grandly across his middle.

Lavinia's sister Minnie was her bridesmaid
and Commodore Nutt had agreed to be the best
man.

As they repeated their vows, the tiny couple looked like living dolls in the great city church. Though they stood straight and tall, both bride and groom reached only to the minister's waist. But this was no show. It was a true wedding of two young people who loved each other.

The next day newspapers called it a "genteel and graceful wedding." They called Lavinia a "Miniature Queen of Beauty," a "Fairy Bride." They said of Tom Thumb that "Next to Napoleon, no one person in our time is better known to high and low, rich and poor."

All marveled at the wedding cake, which Phineas Barnum had ordered. It weighed eighty pounds and towered over the bride as she cut the first slice. Topped with a sugar bride and groom, it was covered with angels, cupids, scrolls, harps, bells, and clusters of rosebuds. It was also delicious. "A True Miracle of the Baker's Art," said the papers.

For the party which followed the wedding, Tom had a surprise of his own. He and Vinnie didn't want to end this happy day with stiff necks. So they received their two thousand wedding guests standing on top of a grand piano! What could have been more sensible?

The reception at the Metropolitan Hotel.

From this height the bride and groom looked right at their friends and spoke to them face-to-face.

From the piano top, like the showman he had been not so long ago, Tom waved his hand for quiet. People hushed their chatter to hear his words; Phineas came closer to listen. What would Tom say, he wondered. What was there left to say?

"Ladies and gentlemen," Tom began in the old way. "I thank you for helping to make this the happiest day of our lives, Lavinia's and mine. The world has been good to us, and we thank you all. I especially thank my best friend in all the world, Mr. Phineas Barnum. He taught me much. Better still, he always called me 'diminutive,' instead of 'little.' He made me feel as big as anybody."

Tom took a deep breath and continued. "I have one more thing to say. Today I seem to have lost my dislike for the word 'little.' Since Lavinia and I have found each other, we do not feel 'little' at all. Instead, we have discovered that we are exactly the right size!"

CHAPTER
6

On their honeymoon Mr. and Mrs. Tom Thumb traveled to Washington. There they visited the White House. President and Mrs. Abraham Lincoln were glad of the break from the horrible Civil War. They sat on a sofa and lifted up the tiny bride and groom to sit between them. President Lincoln was an extremely tall man. "You and I," he told Tom with a twinkle, "are the long and short of it, I guess."

When the couple returned to Bridgeport, they found Tom's little apartment waiting. Tom would stretch out on his red plush sofa, smoking his Dutch pipe, and Vinnie would play the piano sweetly. They'd planned to settle down and quit show business, but not long after the wedding, they were on the road again.

Partly because they enjoyed being together,

Barnum was able to persuade Vinnie and Tom and Minnie and the Commodore to travel together. They would sing and dance, joke and act in little plays for new audiences. Tom's coach and ponies traveled with them, first north to New England and Canada and then to the South. They even went to the American West, which was far from easy to reach in those days.

Later the quartet sailed across the Atlantic. Vinnie, Minnie, and the Commodore had never been abroad before, but many people in the audiences had been children when Tom paid his visits to Europe. "Have you seen our Tom Thumb?" they asked each other. "Why, I can remember when he was a midget child. Now he is a little man with a beard and a wife. There are *four* Little People this time! They look like dolls!"

But, of course, the midgets weren't dolls at all. They grew tired of being stared at. They didn't like causing traffic jams whenever they appeared. So, after two or three years, they returned to America. It was certainly time, Vinnie and Tom decided again, to retire from the stage.

For a while they lived in Tom's tiny apartment in Bridgeport. It was still attached to the house he had built for his parents when he was nine years old. Sometimes they visited Vinnie's hometown of Middleboro, Massachusetts. There they had built a home all their own.

It was, on the outside, a fine three-story house like any other. Inside, doorways and rooms were of normal size. But windows reached to the floor, so little people could look out easily. Stairs had risers to fit short legs. Kitchen shelves were low. The stove was child size because Vinnie liked to cook for her husband.

Here they could live comfortably. Their beautiful wedding gifts were everywhere: beds and sofas, firescreens and tea sets, clocks and footstools; even a tiny billiard table and the rosewood piano. All had been specially made.

Only one room held furniture to fit friends of normal size. Vinnie and Tom had many visitors of this kind. Some were clearly curious as to how such little people lived from day to day. One lady complained because she was entertained in this large room with large furniture. She had expected the whole house and everything in it to be miniature.

"I had hoped," she told her hostess, "to see your pretty *little* things. Maybe to drink tea from cups given you by the king of France. And to sit on a chair chosen by Queen Victoria herself."

Lavinia, from her own low velvet chair, smiled up at the outspoken lady. "Tom and I have some large furniture in our home just for folks like you," she said. "Also doorways are made especially high so two of our best friends from the American Museum can visit us. They are giants eight feet tall."

The lady began to look a bit embarrassed. Why had she not thought of these practical matters?

"Besides, madame," Lavinia continued softly, "those little cups you speak of would hold only a sip of tea for you." Being a lady, Vinnie did *not* add, "And even if you could squeeze into a little chair, it would surely break under your weight."

Still, living quietly grew tiresome, and Tom spent money quickly. Barnum persuaded Lavinia and Tom, Minnie, and Commodore Nutt to travel again. This time they made a "TOM THUMB TOUR AROUND THE WORLD." They went to China and Japan, Australia and Ceylon, India and Egypt.

This journey held both adventure and hardship. The four Little People were amazingly cheerful and brave. For three years they rode in stagecoaches and on trains. They rocked along on camel and donkey back, even on an elephant or two. Sometimes they walked for miles or waded through muddy streams. They climbed steep mountain trails and were caught in desert dust storms. They ate strange foods that sometimes made them ill. They slept in palaces, tents, and dingy inns. In one of these, Lavinia caught a thief who was stealing her jewel case. Another time they barely escaped from a hotel fire.

Always there were servants and piles of luggage to think about. Such luggage! It took many trunks to carry all the necessary costumes and clothing. On state occasions Tom must wear his frock coat and ruffled vest. He set a gold-rimmed monocle in one eye, draped his watch chain grandly across his round little stomach, and wore a huge diamond ring.

At dinner parties on the other side of the world, Vinnie dressed in ball gowns trimmed with ropes of pearls. Also, like other fine ladies of her time, she wore long white gloves as she ate. She had only a few pairs and could not buy others. New gloves had to be made especially for her tiny hands.

Everywhere they went, the four Little People were wildly greeted, even by people who could not understand a word they said. Maharajahs and kings welcomed them. Eager audiences paid large sums of money just to see the tiny couples and touch them, if possible. For in many lands there is a saying that to touch a midget brings good luck.

They sang and danced their way around the world, then home again to the village of Middleboro. It had been an exhausting trip, in a time when few other people had ever tried such a journey. Vinnie's journal says it was a happy time, on the whole a grand adventure.

Tom had always been happiest, he himself wrote, when entertaining children—English, Japanese, Indian, or Ceylonese, it did not matter. He sometimes said wistfully, "I have had a charmed life. But, come to think of it, I never had time to be a child myself." Which, in a way, was true. Since not-quite five years old, Tom Thumb had been a star, working almost every day.

Mr. and Mrs. Thumb lived happily together

for twenty years. Tom died after a short illness in 1883. He was forty-five years old. His grave is in the Mountain Grove Cemetery in Bridge-port, Connecticut, the town where he was born. As you look at the statue on top of its tall marble monument, it is easy to imagine that General Tom Thumb is about to bow grandly and say,

Good evening, ladies and gentlemen!

A NOTE FROM THE AUTHOR

If denied the pleasure of seeing Tom Thumb, a nine-teenth-century admirer could read about him, sing his songs from sheet music, and dance quadrilles choreographed in his name. The *Tiny Library*, a series of miniature books with such titles as *The Life of General Tom Thumb* and *The Lives of Tom Thumb and His Lady*, was published in various editions (in London, New York, and Philadelphia) from 1849 to 1881.

Whenever possible, I availed myself of these nineteenth-century sources. I found a glowing description of Lavinia's wedding gown in the May 1863 issue of *Godey's Lady's Book*, and, of course, *Harper's Weekly* was often filled with news and feature stories about Tom's adventures.

Phineas T. Barnum himself left nine autobiographical volumes. Their very titles bespeak this man of enormous ego and charm, from the first, *The Autobiography of Petite Bunkum, the Showman, Written by Himself*, published in 1855, to the last, *Funny Stories*, published in 1890. Barnum often disagreed with details from his own earlier accounts about Tom Thumb; he, more than anyone, was aware of Tom's life as a legend in the making. We may never know just who gave Tom his red, white, and blue coach, or how the boy actually traveled when he first came to New York City. Lavinia Warren Stratton's autobiography, handwritten and unpublished at the time of my research, also contains contradictions on such points.

The Harvard Theatre Collection was a valuable source of information, including the texts of Tom Thumb's letters, re-produced here. I was unable to find the original invitations proffered by Barnum and Queen Victoria (chapter three) and have imagined their contents. The dialogue, too, is mostly invented, but readers may be assured that Tom Thumb's wedding speech was widely reported, just as quoted here.

In a real sense, Phineas Barnum and Charles Sherwood Stratton "made" each other. Both were aware of the mutual bond. Still, the friendship between these two seems to have been a true one, not based on expediency or gratitude alone. Much has been written about the hordes of people who flocked to see the beloved midget. The nineteenth century was a simpler time than ours; still, after much research, I feel certain that these people were not hoodwinked by Barnum's ballyhoo. They took Tom Thumb to their hearts because he was bright, talented, and gifted with a winning nature. In this spirit, I wanted to introduce him here, to the children of the twentieth century.

Helen Reeder Cross
Hastings-on-Hudson,
New York

If you go to Bridgeport, Connecticut, you may want to visit the Barnum Museum on 820 Main Street, at the corner of Main and Gilbert. It contains much Tom Thumb memorabilia as well as "the foremost miniature circus in the world," W. R. Brinley's 5-Ring Circus. Open Tuesdays through Saturdays from 12-5 PM and on Sundays from 2-5 PM, the building was designed, in part, by P.T. Barnum, who gave it as a gift to the city of Bridgeport. Barnum was also one of the founders of the Mountain Grove Cemetery, at 2675 North Avenue. Summer hours are from 8 AM to 6 PM; the cemetery closes at 4 PM in the winter.

Grace Church, where Mr. and Mrs. Tom Thumb were married, stands at 800 Broadway, on the northeast corner of East 10th Street in New York City. The tower, especially, is beautiful to see.